Fun Food to Make

Written by Kerrie Shanahan

Photography by Michael Curtain

Flying Start
to Literacy®

Contents

Introduction

This book has recipes that are fun to make.

The foods in these recipes will help you to stay active and healthy.

 This chef's hat means an adult needs to help you.

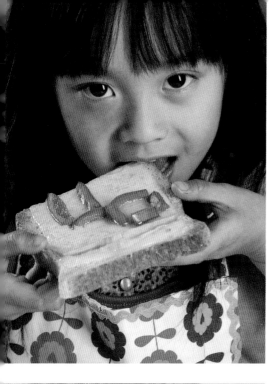

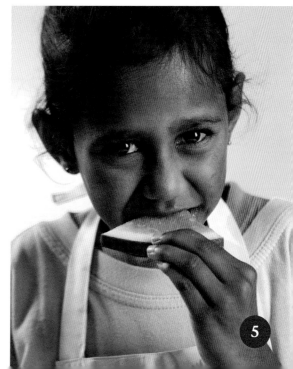

Pizza face

You will need:

1 pita bread

1 tablespoon of tomato paste

1 cup of grated cheese

1 cup of shredded ham

1 slice of pineapple

1 cherry tomato

1 mushroom

What to do:

1. Spread tomato paste over the pita bread.

2. Sprinkle grated cheese over the tomato paste.

3. Cut the tomato down the middle. Put it on the pizza to make the eyes on the pizza face.

4. Put the shredded ham on the pizza to make it look like hair.

5. Cut the mushroom into a triangle.

6. Put the mushroom on the pizza face to make it look like a nose.

7. Cut the pineapple so that it looks like a smiley mouth. Put it on the pizza.

8. Cook it in a hot oven for 10–15 minutes.

Try this ...

Use a rice cake and add grated carrot hair, a lettuce mouth and olive eyes.

Apple boat

You will need:

1 slice of watermelon

1 apple

1 toothpick

Try this ...

Make a boat out of an orange and give it a pineapple sail.

What to do:

1. Cut the apple down the middle.

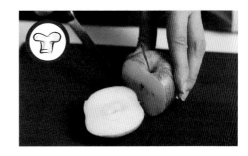

2. Put a toothpick in the middle of the apple.

3. Cut a triangle shape out of the watermelon.

4. Put the watermelon triangle on the toothpick to make a sail.

Bread person

You will need:

1 slice of bread

1 tablespoon of honey

5 sultanas

1 dried apricot

1 person-shaped cookie cutter

Try this ...

Put cream cheese, corn and tomato on your bread person.

What to do:

1. Cut the bread into the shape of a person with the cookie cutter.

2. Spread the honey onto the bread person.

3. Put the sultanas on the bread to make them look like eyes and buttons.

4. Cut the dried apricot into thin strips and put an apricot strip on the bread to make it look like a mouth.

Cheesy house

You will need:

1 slice of bread

1 slice of cheese

1 slice of ham

1 red capsicum

What to do:

1. Toast one side of the bread under a grill.

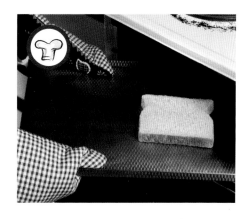

2. Put the slice of cheese on the uncooked side of the bread.

3. Cut the capsicum into thin strips.

4. Put the capsicum
strips on the cheese
to make them look
like a door and
a window.

5. Cut the ham
into a triangle.

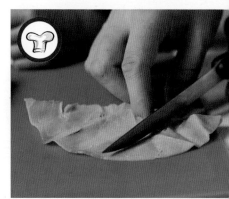

6. Put it on top of the cheese to look like a roof.

7. Put the bread under the grill. Cook it until the cheese melts.

Try this ...

Place a cheesy house on a plate. Add carrot sticks to make a fence and a boiled egg to make a sun.

Tasty rocket

You will need:

1 slice of watermelon

3 grapes

3 strawberries

1 skewer

What to do:

1. Cut a slice of watermelon into one large triangle and one smaller triangle.

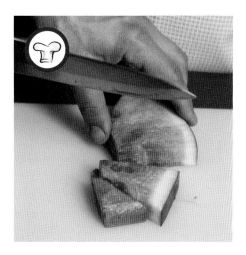

2. Put the large watermelon triangle onto the skewer.

3. Put the grapes
and strawberries
onto the skewer
until they almost
reach the end.

4. Place the smaller
watermelon triangle
onto the end of
the skewer.

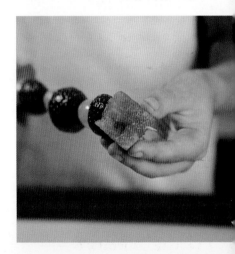

Try this ...

Dip your rocket into yoghurt
before eating.